W9-BYZ-115

CHRONICLE BOOKS
SAN FRANCISCO

HEY, YOU!

YES, YOU.

THE AWESOME PERSON READING THIS BOOK.

YOU ARE SO LOVED.

It's something we could all stand to be reminded of from time to time. Maybe the boy we have a crush on doesn't like us back. Maybe we're not getting along with a friend or relative. No matter. The world is big and, contrary to what they'd have you believe on the news, full of love. Maybe it's the city you live in that loves you back. Maybe it's the artist you'll never meet who puts up a mural to tell you that "you are nature's greatest miracle." The ability to accept the love the world is giving you is a rare and valuable gift.

A couple of years back a little book snuck out into the world called *Everything Is Going to Be OK*. A small, happy, hopeful volume, it was dedicated to the proposition that people were ready for a little hope, a little joy, a little positivity in their lives. Around that time, a number of artists had started putting bold words of affirmation into their work, and that book was a celebration of those brave souls and the astonishing, encouraging, and beautiful images they were making across all kinds of media. We surmised that folks might like this sort of thing—and boy, oh boy, do they ever! The response that book has gotten has been nothing short of humbling. Quite simply, it makes people happy.

And so we are beyond honored to bring you another collection of audaciously positive art, craft, photography, and design. One of the most important things creative people do is make their viewpoint manifest in the world—to publicly enact their slantwise vision. In the case of the intrepid artists in this book, that means standing up and being counted as one of the ones full of warmth, full of affection, full of—yes—love for their fellow creatures. We owe it to them, and to ourselves, to cultivate our own gifts of receptivity—to accept the magic and sanguinity they offer, to let them make us smile, and then to turn around and reflect that love on the people around us. You won't regret it.

THE FUTURE IS NOW

IT WILL BE MORE BEAUTIFUL THAN YOU COULD EVER IMAGINE

WHAT TO FOCUS ON:

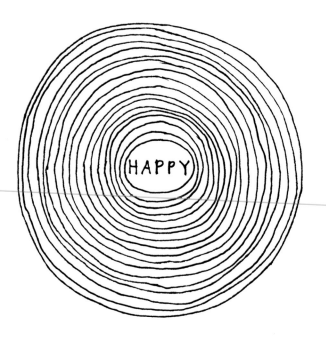

marc johns

LOVED & WANTED

here & now

we are shiny and bright

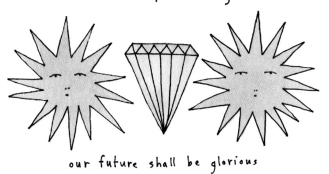

our future shall be glorious

marc johns

TODAY IS THE GREATEST

KEEP YOUR CHIN UP!

CONCEIVE BELIEVE ACHIEVE

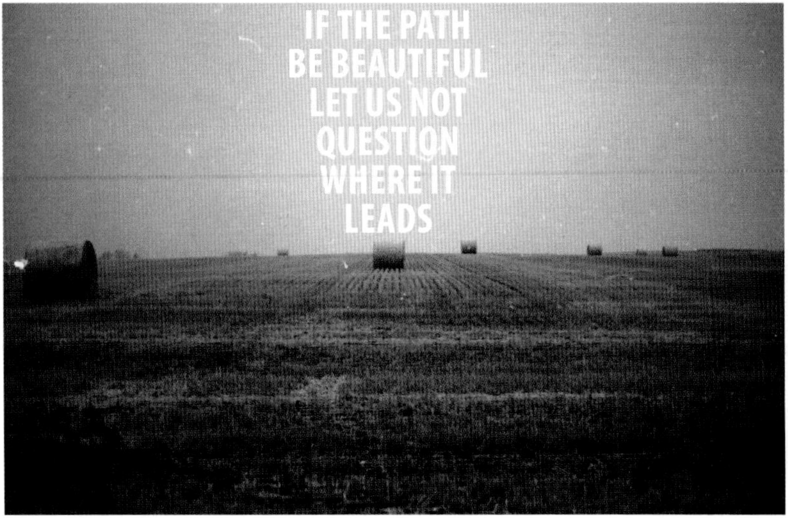

IF THE PATH
BE BEAUTIFUL
LET US NOT
QUESTION
WHERE IT
LEADS

ILL CALL YOU LEWIS IF YOU CALL ME CLARK

This is where it's beautiful

Gx

I'M SO HAPPY
WE BOTH
SHOWED UP HERE.

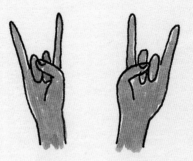

LET'S PRETEND TO ROCK

marc johns

life is a song

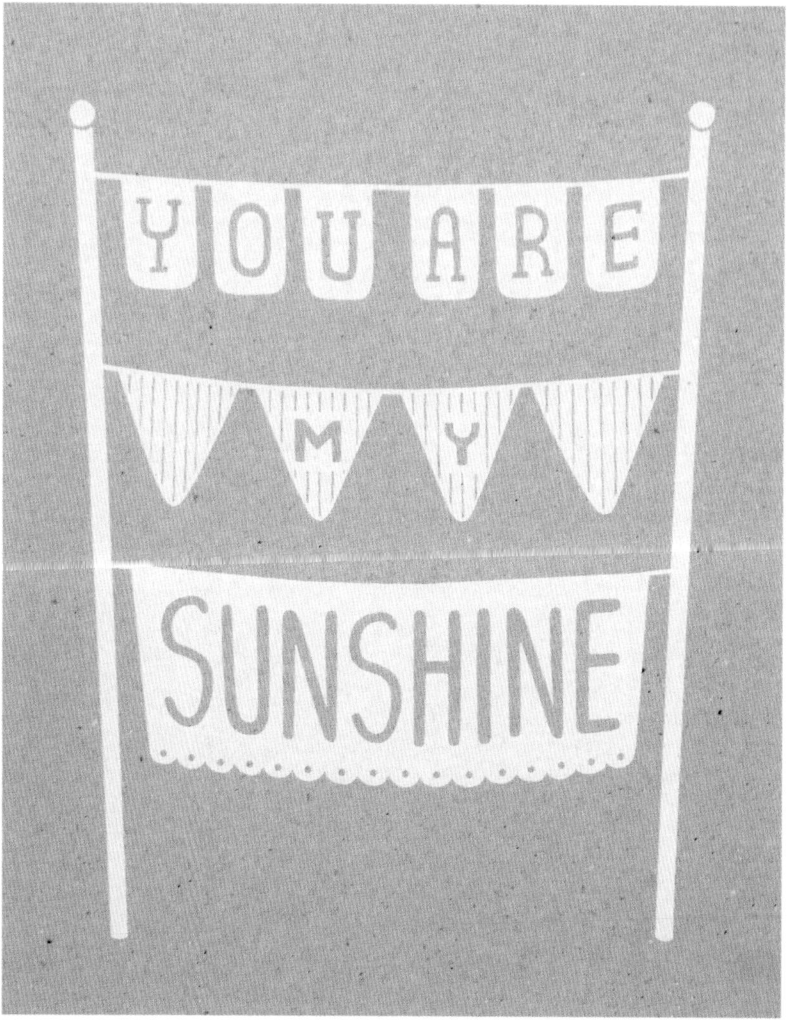
YOU ARE
MY
SUNSHINE

sweet

sweet

LOVE

is all you

need

i s in
ever
FOR

G
Thing YOU

Cx

Love is

re and to let be

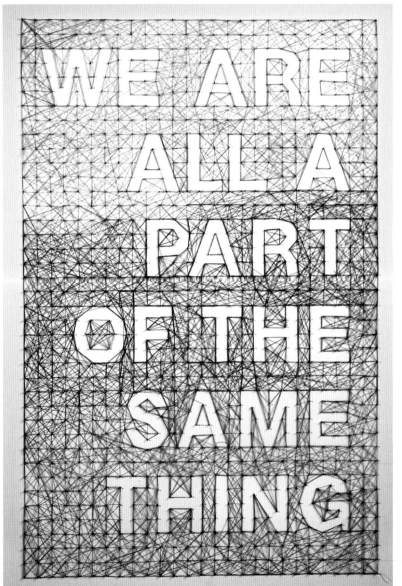

NOBODY'S PERFCET

Everything is ok.

✸✸✸✸   www.kennedyprints.com   ✸✸✸✸
Kennedy Prints!   P.O. Box 650   Gordo, AL 35466

KEEP Your CHIN UP

CLAUDE THINKS YOU LOOK
LOVELY TODAY.

RISE & SHINE

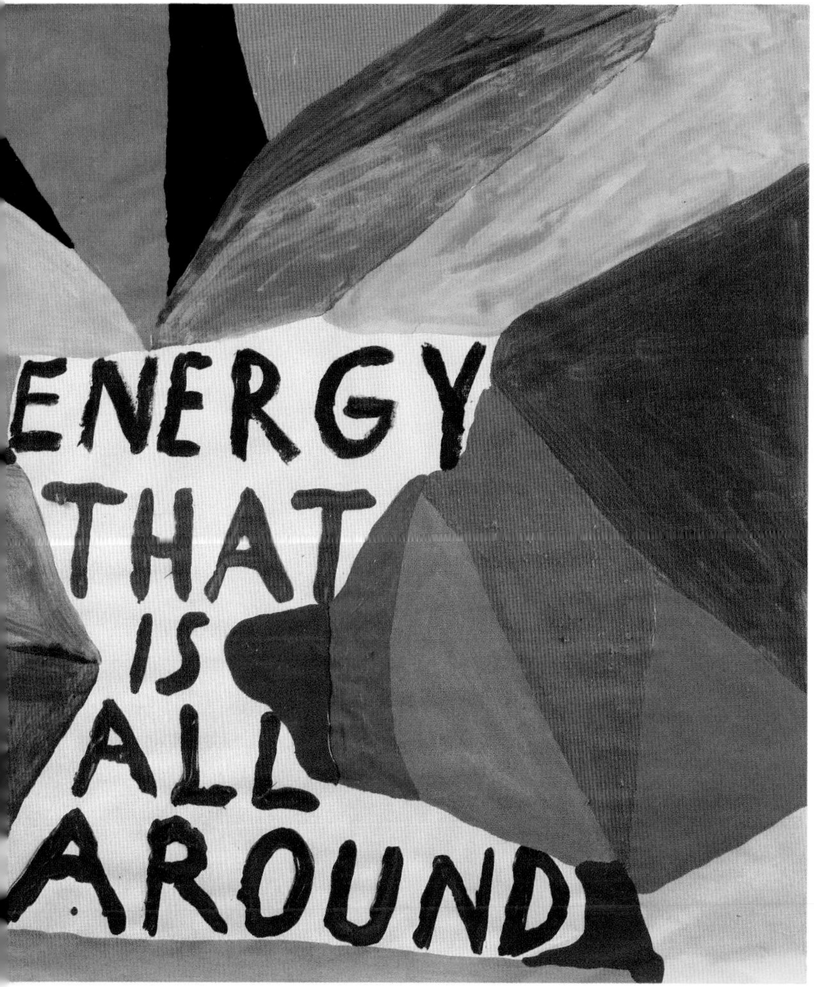
ENERGY
THAT
IS
ALL
AROUND

LIFE IS A MERRY GO ROUND

IT'S NICE TO BE
IMPORTANT BUT
IT'S MORE IMPORT-
ANT TO BE REALLY
REALLY NICE.

YOU
deserve
GOOD
THINGS.

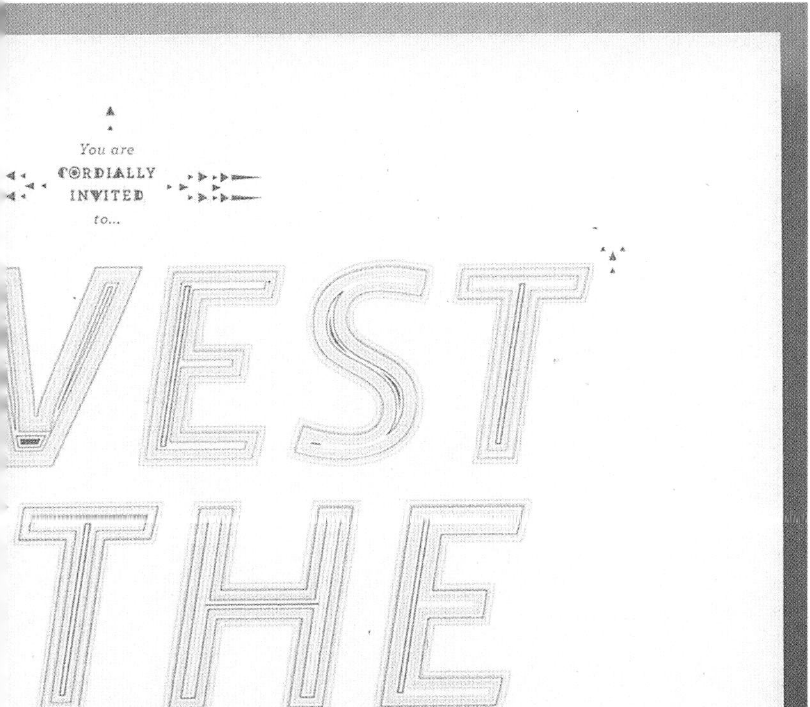

You are
CORDIALLY
INVITED
to...

VEST
THE
ASTIC

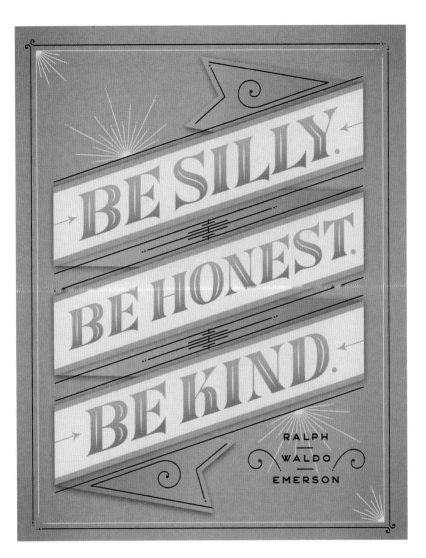

BE SILLY.
BE HONEST.
BE KIND.

RALPH WALDO EMERSON

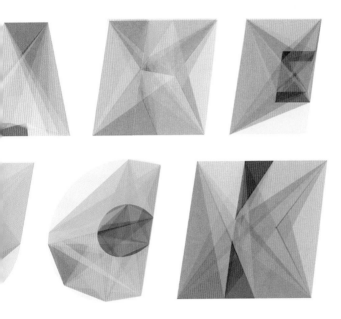

ONE DAY THIS WILL ALL MAKE SENSE TO YOU

magic

You're magic!

YOU ARE MY FAVORITE PERSON IN THE WHOLE WORLD. AND THAT INCLUDES THE IMAGINARY ONES.

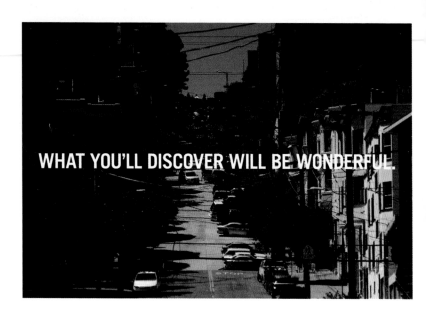

WHAT YOU'LL DISCOVER WILL BE WONDERFUL.

You are
CORDIALLY
INVITED
to...

BE

COURAGEOUS

AND

VULNERABLE

I THINK
YOU'RE
lovely
(IT'S TRUE)

IMAGE CREDITS